CHART PATTERNS & CANDLESTICK PATTERNS IN STOCK MARKET TRADING

CHART PATTERNS & CANDLESTICK PATTERNS

IN STOCK MARKET TRADING

INDRAZITH SHANTHARAJ

AMARYLLIS
BUSINESS
An imprint of Manjul Publishing House

AMARYLLIS
BUSINESS

An imprint of Manjul Publishing House Pvt. Ltd.
• C-16, Sector 3, Noida, Uttar Pradesh 201301, India
Website: www.manjulindia.com
Registered Office:
• 2nd Floor, Usha Preet Complex,
42, Malviya Nagar, Bhopal 462 003 - India
Distribution Centres
Ahmedabad, Bengaluru, Chennai, Hyderabad,
Kochi, Kolkata, Mumbai, Noida, Pune

Chart Patterns & Candlestick Patterns in Stock Market Trading
by Indrazith Shantharaj

This edition first published in 2024
Third impression 2026

ISBN 978-93-5543-516-3

Printed and bound in India by Saurabh Printers Pvt. Ltd.

Contents

Disclaimer 7

Acknowledgment 9

Trading Chart Pattern 11

- #1 Head and Shoulder Pattern 14
- #2 Inverse Head and Shoulder Pattern 18
- #3 Double Top Pattern 22
- #4 Double Bottom Pattern 26
- #5 Triple Top Pattern 30
- #6 Triple Bottom Pattern 34
- #7 Cup & Handle Pattern 38
- #8 Inverted Cup & Handle Pattern 42
- #9 Bull Flag Pattern 46
- #10 Bear Flag Pattern 50
- #11 Symmetrical Triangle Pattern 54
- #12 Rising Wedge Pattern 59

Candlestick Patterns 63

#1 Bullish Engulfing Pattern 63

#2 Bearish Engulfing Pattern 65

#3 Marubozu Pattern 67

#4 Pinbar Pattern 70

#5 Doji Pattern 73

A Word of Caution! 77

The Importance of Money Management 81

The Importance of Trading Psychology 83

Disclaimer

This book is sold with the understanding that the author is not engaged in rendering legal, accounting, or any kind of advice while publishing this book. Each individual's risk appetite and expectations from the market are different.

All ideas, opinions expressed or implied herein, information, charts, or examples contained in the lessons are for informational and educational purposes only. They should not be constructed as a recommendation to invest and trade in the market. The author disclaims any liability, loss, or risk resulting, directly or indirectly, from using or applying any book's contents.

Technical analysis is a study of past performance, and past performance does not guarantee future performance. Investors and traders are advised to take the services of a competent expert before making any investment or trading decision.

Acknowledgment

Many helped in the preparation of this book. I want to thank all my Trading Gurus who taught me everything about trading.

I want to thank the Tradingview Team, as all the charts in this book are taken from their website.

Many traders helped me immensely to spread awareness about my books. They are Sanket Gajjar, Harneet Singh, Rachit Jain, Swapnaja Sharma, Chetan Kumar, Nataraj Malavade, and Vinay Kumar. More power to you guys!

Thanks to Nadini Panchakshari, who helped with editing and proofreading.

I have many friends who have supported me in all my book ventures. I will be forever grateful to all of them.

Indrazith Shantharaj
Sep 2023

Trading Chart Pattern

At any point in time, a trader will:

1. Aim to take a NEW TRADE
2. Book Profit/Loss for an EXISTING TRADE
3. Planning TRIAL STOP-LOSS for an existing trade

The knowledge of chart patterns will help immensely to perform all the actions mentioned above in the market in any timeframe.

These chart patterns hold significant importance for traders (both beginners and intermediate-level traders) in the financial markets.

Here are several reasons why they are essential:

1. **Visualization of Market Psychology**: Chart patterns represent market psychology and people's behavior. They reflect the collective sentiment and decision-making of all the market participants. By studying these patterns, traders can gain significant insights into the emotions and beliefs driving market movements, such as fear, greed, optimism, or pessimism.

2. **Price Action Analysis**: Chart patterns provide helpful information about price action, which is a stock's price movement over time. Traders can identify patterns such as trends, reversals, or consolidations, helping them understand the current state of the market and anticipate potential future price movements.
3. **Entry and Exit Points**: Chart patterns can effectively identify optimal entry and exit points in trades. For example, a trader may locate a bullish pattern indicating an upward trend and use it as a signal or confirmation to enter a long trade. Similarly, a bearish pattern could show a potential fall, prompting a trader to exit a long trade or consider shorting a position.
4. **Risk Management**: Chart patterns assist in managing risk by providing traders with possible stop-loss levels and profit targets. By identifying support and resistance levels within patterns, traders can set appropriate risk-reward ratios and adjust their position sizes accordingly.
5. **Confirmation of Trade Setups**: Chart patterns can be an additional confirmation tool for other trading indicators or strategies. When people notice a chart pattern aligning with their technical analysis, it strengthens their conviction in a trade setup and increases the likelihood of a successful trade.

In summary, trading chart patterns provide traders with valuable insights into market psychology, price action, and potential trade setups.

By studying and understanding these chart patterns, traders can enhance their decision-making, improve risk management, and increase their chances of success in the stock markets.

#1 Head and Shoulder Pattern

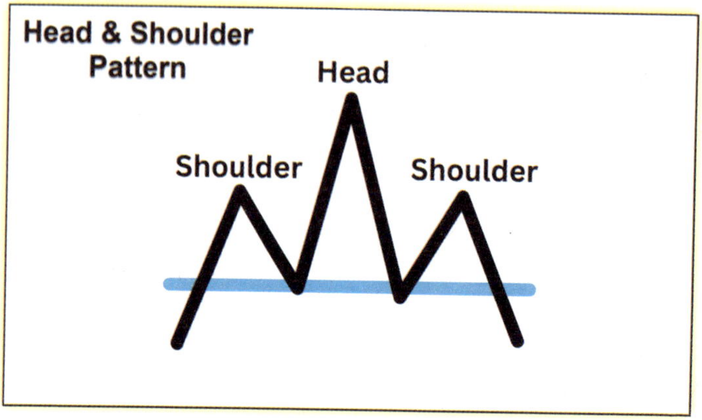

The Head and Shoulders pattern in technical analysis is a simple chart pattern that typically denotes a reversal in a trend.

It consists of 3 peaks, with the middle peak being the highest (known as "head"), flanked by two lower peaks (known as "shoulders").

This pattern indicates that an uptrend is likely to reverse into a downtrend, and traders often use it as a signal to sell their existing long positions or take short positions.

How to Trade Head & Shoulder Pattern?

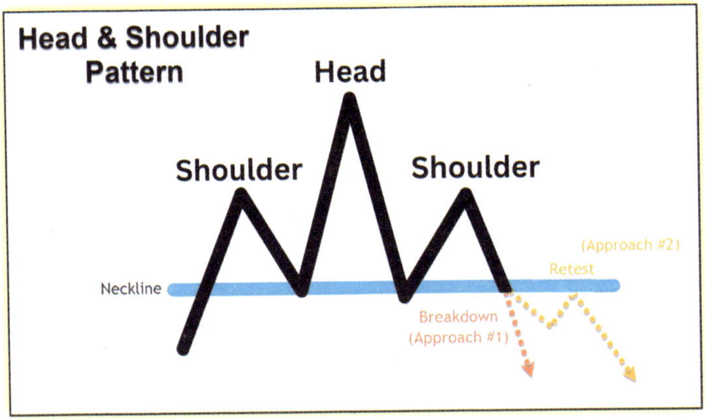

Approach #1 – Directly taking a short trade when the price breaks the neckline (risky, but you will be in trade every time).

Approach #2 – Plan short trades only when the price goes back, test the neckline, and fail to trade above it (less risk, but you may miss the trade if the price doesn't retest the neckline).

In both cases, we can aim the height of the head from the neckline as our target.

Few Examples of Head & Shoulder Pattern

Image - H&S Pattern in HDFC

Image - H&S Pattern in TCS

Image - H&S Pattern in Power Finance Corp

Image - H&S Pattern in GAIL

#2 Inverse Head and Shoulder Pattern

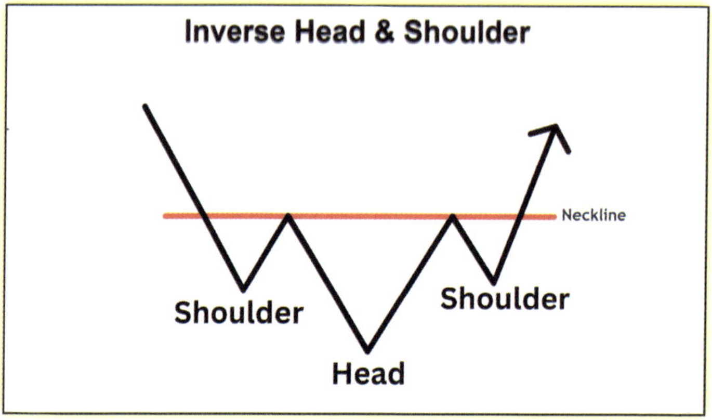

The Inverse Head and Shoulders pattern is similar to the Head and Shoulder pattern but in the opposite direction.

It consists of three elements - the middle curve being the lowest (the "head") and the two higher curves on both sides (the "shoulders").

This pattern indicates that a downtrend might reverse into an uptrend, and traders often use this as an indication to close their existing short positions or take new long positions.

How to Trade Inverse Head & Shoulder Pattern?

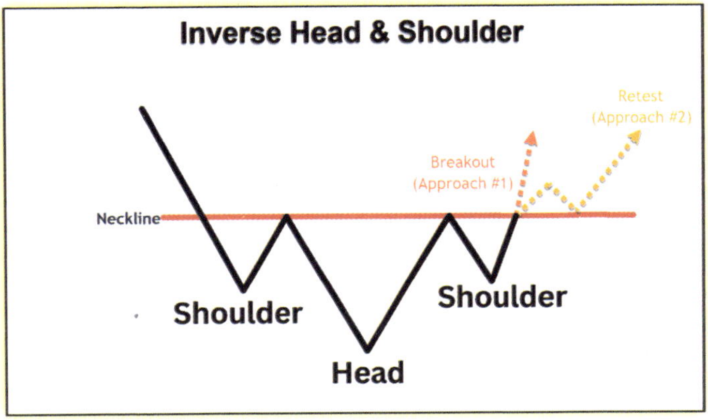

Approach #1 – Directly taking a Long trade when the price breaks the neckline (risky, but you will be in trade every time).

Approach #2 – Plan Long trades only when the price comes back, test the neckline, and fail to break it (less risk, but you may miss the trade if the price doesn't retest the neckline).

In both cases, we can aim the height of the head from the neckline as our target.

Few Examples of Inverse Head & Shoulder Pattern

Image – Inverse H&S Pattern in GAIL

Image – Inverse H&S Pattern in CIPLA

Image – Inverse H&S Pattern in Maruti Suzuki

Image – Inverse H&S Pattern in Nestle India

#3 Double Top Pattern

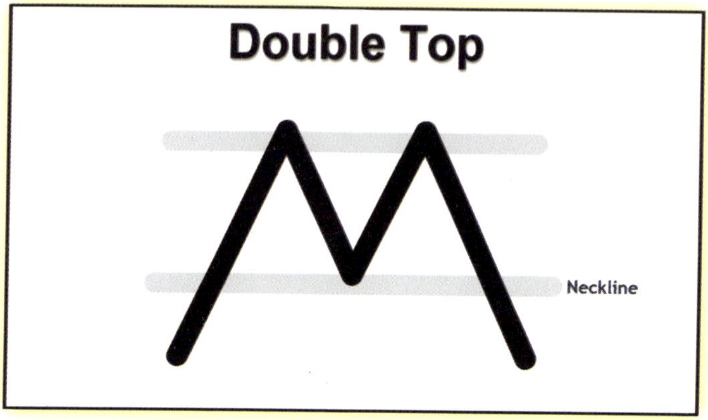

The double top pattern is the simplest chart pattern in trading, often indicating a potential trend reversal (uptrend to downtrend).

It appears as two higher peaks on a price chart, separated by a short decline (a trough), forming a neckline.

This pattern suggests that the party is over in an uptrend, and traders often interpret it as a signal to book profits for their existing long positions and to take short positions, anticipating a shift to a downtrend.

How to Trade Double Top Pattern?

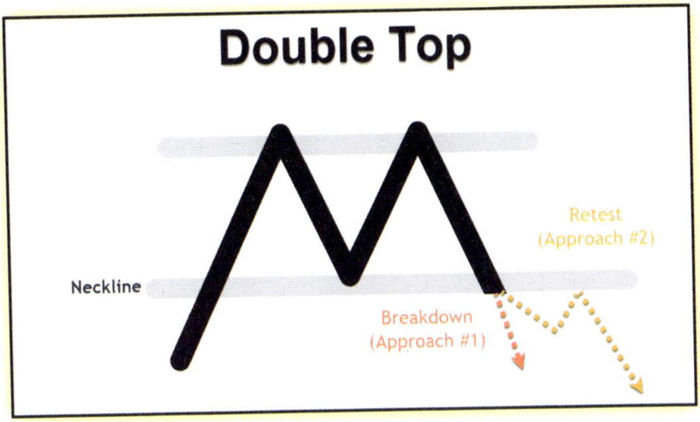

Approach #1 – Directly taking a Short trade when the price breaks the neckline (risky, but you will be in trade every time).

Approach #2 – Plan Short trades only when the price comes back, retests the neckline and fails to trade above it (less risk, but you may miss the trade if the price doesn't retest the neckline).

In both cases, we can aim the height of the double top as our target.

Few Examples of Double Top Pattern

Image – Double Top Pattern in Nifty

Image – Double Top Pattern in BankNifty

Image – Double Top Pattern in ICICI Bank

Image – Double Top Pattern in SBIN

#4 Double Bottom Pattern

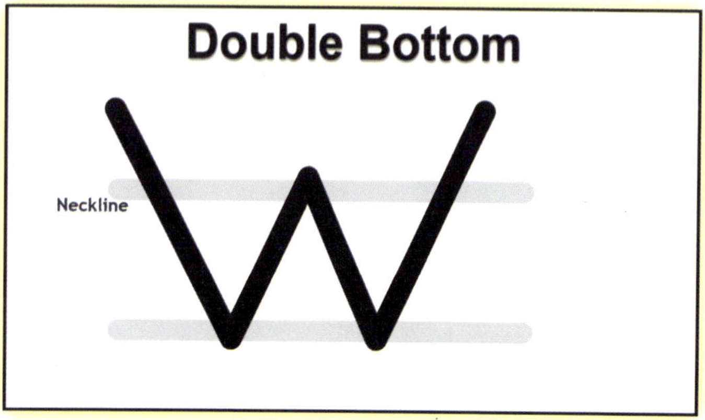

The double bottom pattern is similar to the double top pattern but indicates the reversal from downtrend to uptrend.

It consists of two low points on a price chart, separated by a temporary peak.

This pattern indicates that a downtrend could be ending, and traders plan to opt for new long positions or close their existing short positions.

How to Trade Double Bottom Pattern?

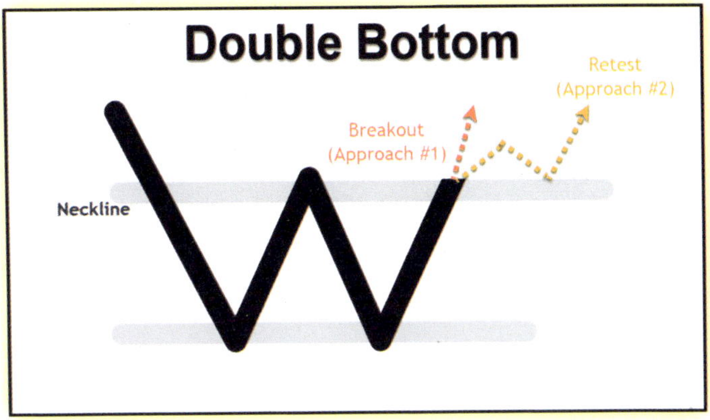

Approach #1 – Directly taking a Long trade when the price breaks the neckline (risky, but you will be in trade every time).

Approach #2 – Plan Long trades only when the price comes back, test the neckline, and fail to break it (less risk, but you may miss the trade if the price doesn't retest the neckline).

In both cases, we can aim for the height of the double bottom as our target.

Few Examples of Double Bottom Pattern

Image – Double Bottom Pattern in Banknifty

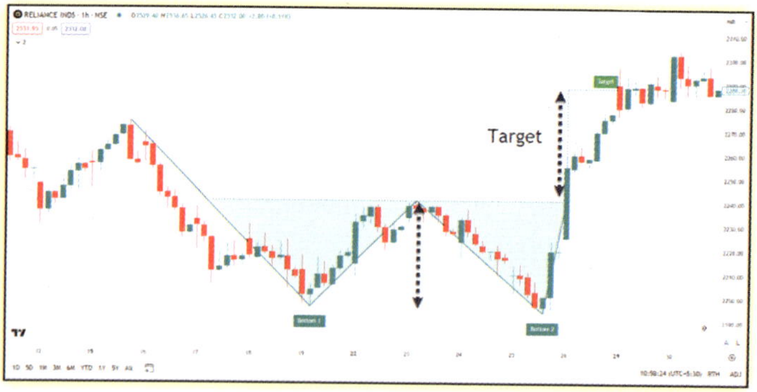

Image – Double Bottom Pattern in Reliance

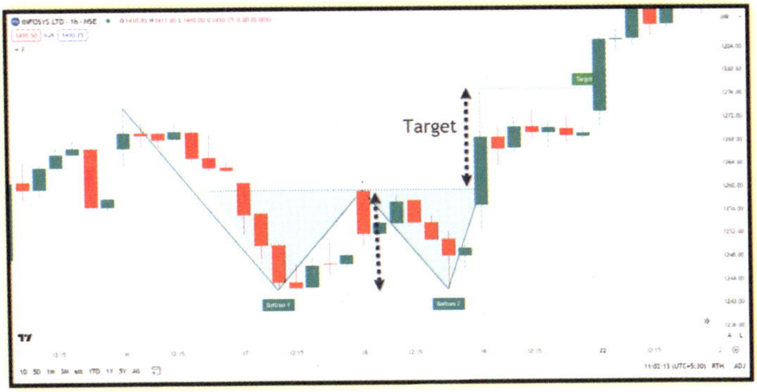

Image – Double Bottom Pattern in Infy

Image – Double Bottom Pattern in TCS

#5 Triple Top Pattern

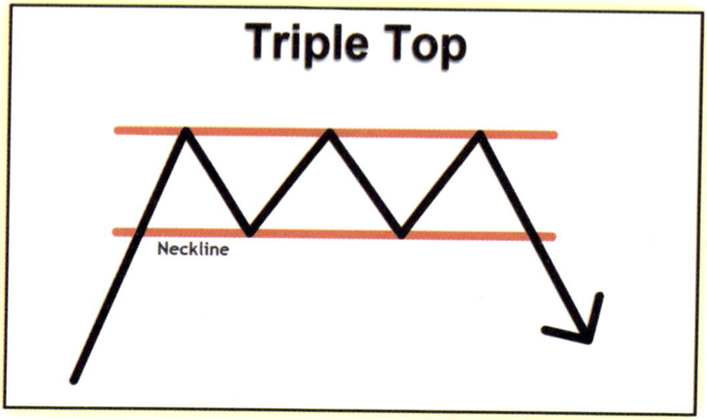

The triple top pattern is a significant chart pattern similar to the double top pattern but with one additional top.

It's characterized by three separate attempts to break through a specific price level (nothing but peaks), followed by a decline each time.

This pattern indicates that an uptrend is losing strength, and traders often interpret it as a signal to close their existing long positions or initiate new short positions, anticipating a shift toward a downtrend.

How to Trade Triple Top Pattern?

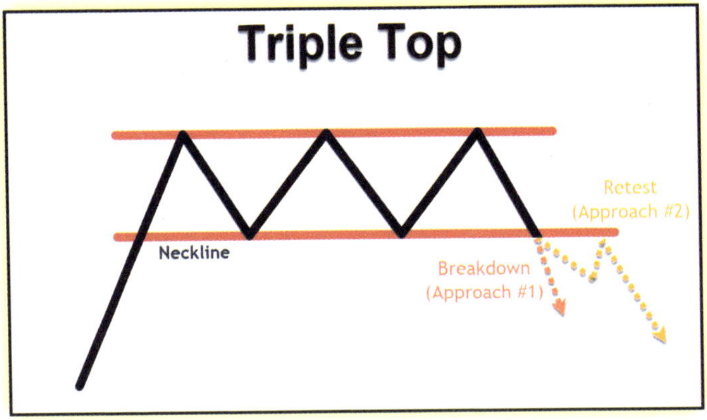

Approach #1 – Directly taking a Short trade when the price breaks the neckline (risky, but you will be in trade every time).

Approach #2 – Plan Short trades only when the price comes back, retests the neckline and fails to trade above it (less risk, but you may miss the trade if the price doesn't retest the neckline).

In both cases, we can aim the height of the triple top as our target.

Few Examples of Triple Top Pattern

Image – Triple Top Pattern in Canara Bank

Image – Triple Top Pattern in Titan

Image – Triple Top Pattern in Grasim

Image – Triple Top Pattern in Bajaj Auto

#6 Triple Bottom Pattern

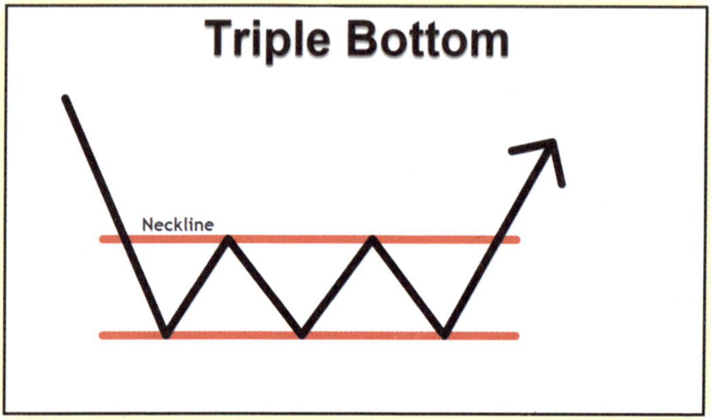

The triple bottom pattern is a notable chart pattern in technical analysis that can indicate a possible trend reversal from downtrend to uptrend.

It involves three distinct instances of reaching similar price lows, followed by a recovery each time.

This pattern suggests that a downtrend might be weakening, and traders often view it as a signal to take new long positions or close their existing short positions, expecting a shift toward an uptrend.

How to Trade Triple Bottom Pattern?

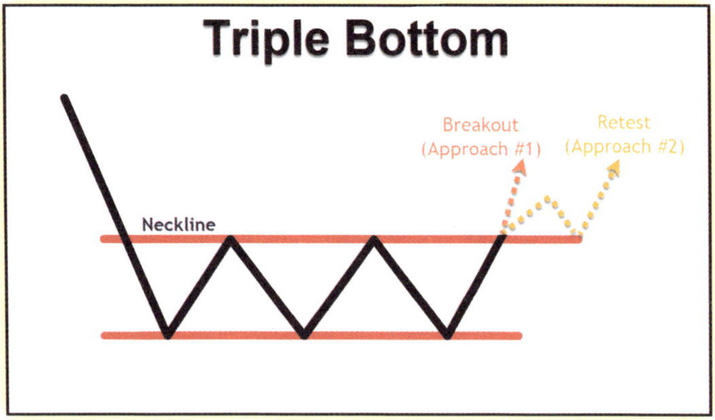

Approach #1 – Directly taking a Long trade when the price breaks the neckline (risky, but you will be in trade every time).
Approach #2 – Plan Long trades only when the price comes back, test the neckline, and fail to break it (less risk, but you may miss the trade if the price doesn't retest the neckline).

In both cases, we can aim the height of the triple bottom as our target.

Few Examples of Triple Bottom Pattern

Image – Triple Bottom Pattern in Cipla

Image – Triple Bottom Pattern in Bharti Airtel

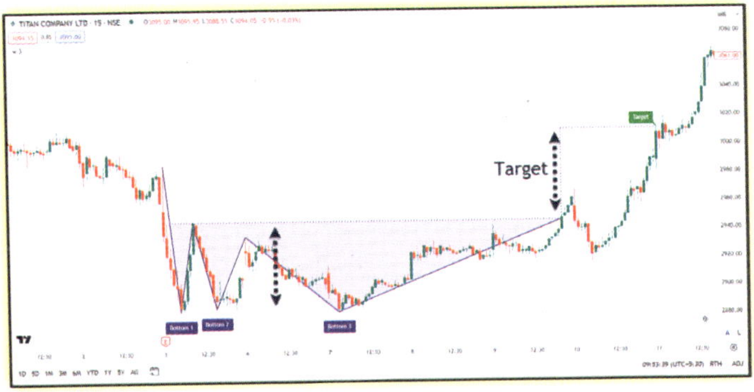

Image – Triple Bottom Pattern in Titan

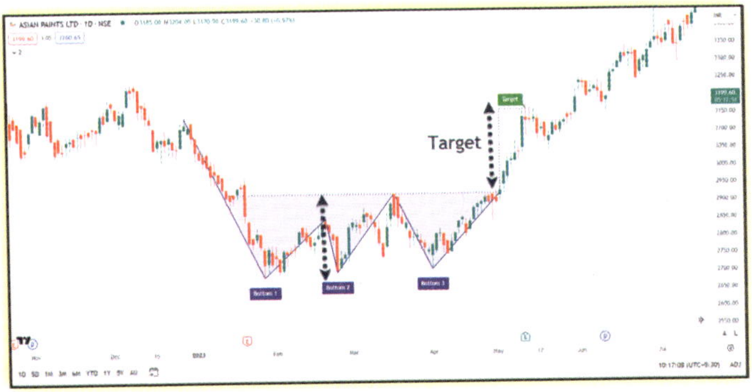

Image – Triple Bottom Pattern in Asian Paints

#7 Cup & Handle Pattern

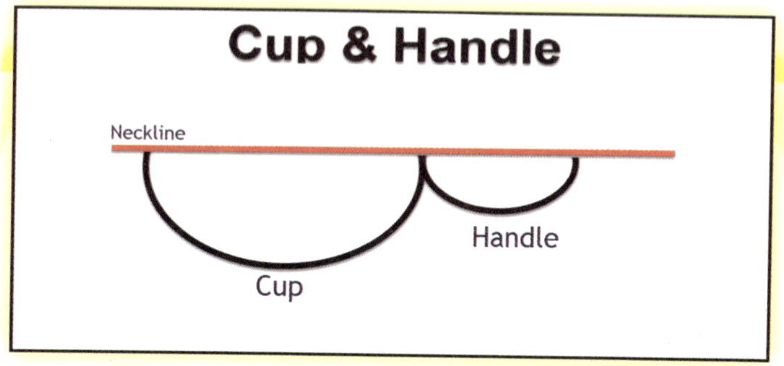

The cup and handle pattern is a simple breakout chart pattern in trading that often signifies the strength of bulls and a potential continuation of an uptrend.

It resembles a **tea cup** with a rounded bottom, a small consolidation, a slight downward pullback, and nothing but the **handle**.

This pattern suggests that after a temporary consolidation, the price would resume its upward movement (high probability).

Traders often interpret it as a signal to buy or add more positions, anticipating the continuation of the uptrend.

How to Trade Cup & Handle Pattern?

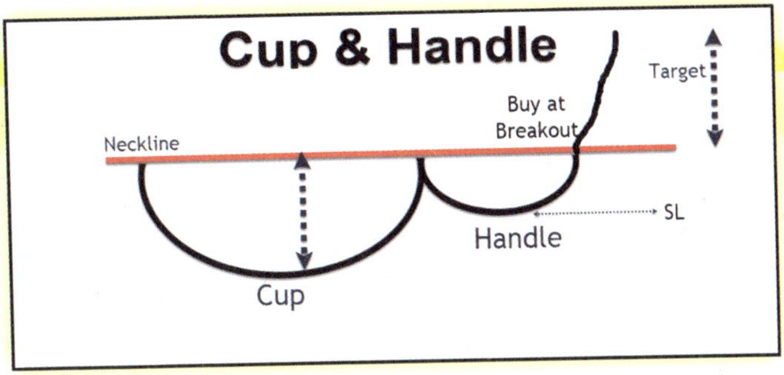

To trade the cup and handle pattern, follow these steps:

- **Identify the Cup**: Look for a rounded bottom on the price chart, forming the cup shape. This part should show a gradual increase followed by a gentle decline.
- **Spot the Handle**: After the cup formation, observe a short consolidation or pullback known as the handle. The handle should be smaller in size compared to the cup.
- **Entry Point**: Plan to enter a trade when the price breaks out above the handle's upper boundary, i.e., neckline. This breakout confirms the pattern's potential continuation.
- **Set Stop-Loss**: Place a stop-loss order below the lowest point of the handle. This helps limit potential losses if the breakout fails.
- **Target Price**: Estimate the target price by measuring the distance from the bottom of the cup to the neckline and adding it to the breakout point. This can give you a rough idea of how far the price might move.

Few Examples of Cup & Handle Pattern

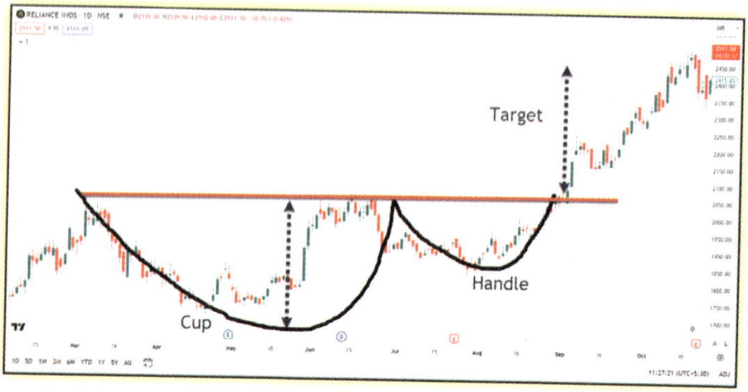

Image – Cup & Handle Pattern in Reliance

Image – Cup & Handle Pattern in Bajaj Finance

Image – Cup & Handle Pattern in HDFC Bank

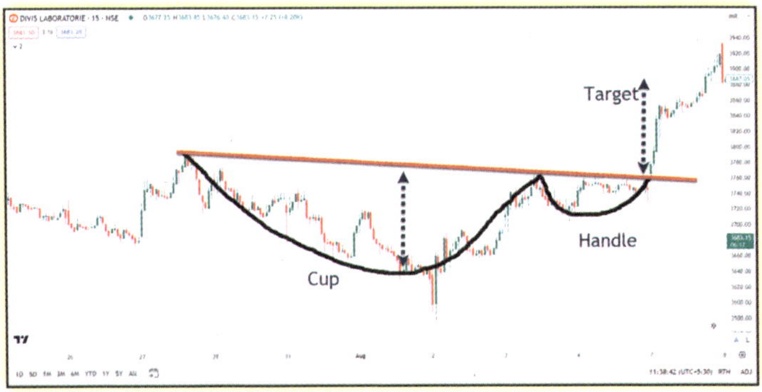

Image – Cup & Handle Pattern in Divis Lab

#8 Inverted Cup & Handle Pattern

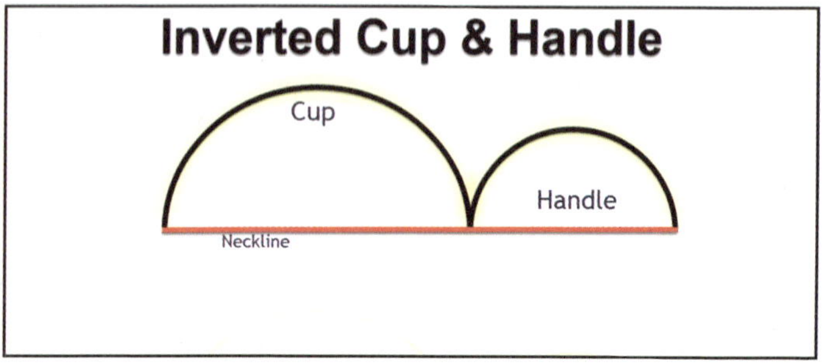

The inverted cup and handle pattern is a trading pattern that often indicates a potential downtrend continuation.

It's the opposite of the regular cup and handle pattern. It features a downward price movement resembling an upside-down tea cup (the inverted cup), followed by a brief consolidation and an upward drift (the handle).

Traders interpret this pattern as a signal to sell, anticipating the downtrend's continuation.

How to Trade Inverted Cup & Handle Pattern?

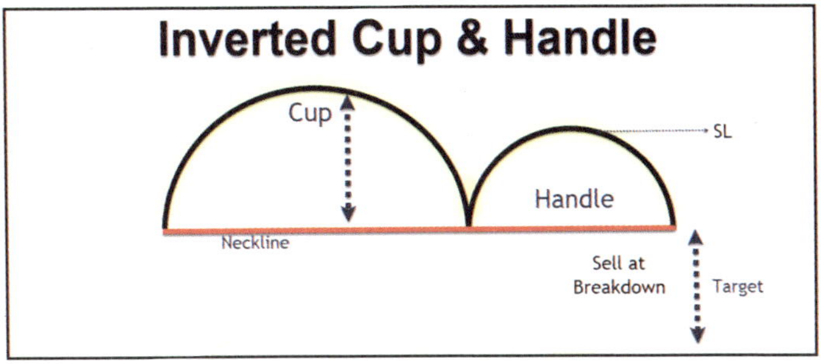

To trade the inverted cup and handle pattern, follow these steps:

- **Identify the Inverted Cup**: Look for a rounded top on the price chart, forming the inverted cup shape.
- **Spot the Inverted Handle**: After the inverted cup formation, observe a short bounce, nothing but the inverted handle. The handle should be smaller in size compared to the cup.
- **Entry Point**: Plan to enter a short trade when the price breaks below the neckline. This breakdown confirms the pattern's potential continuation.
- **Set Stop-Loss**: Place a stop-loss order above the highest point of the handle. This helps limit potential losses if the breakdown fails.
- **Target Price**: Estimate the target price by measuring the distance from the top of the cup to the neckline and adding it to the breakdown point. This can give you a rough idea of how far the price might move.

Few Examples of Inverted Cup & Handle Pattern

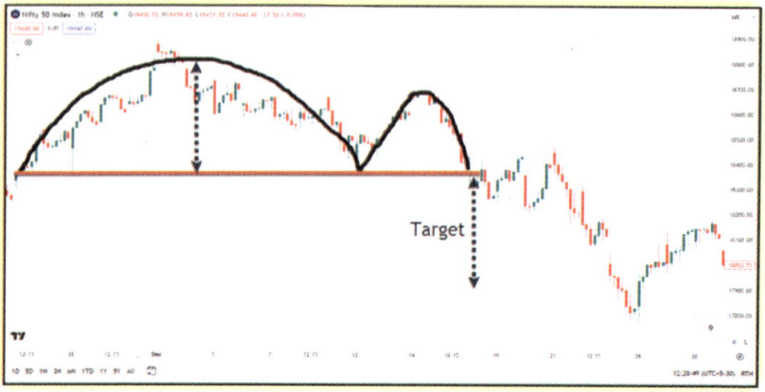

Image – Inverted Cup & Handle Pattern in Nifty

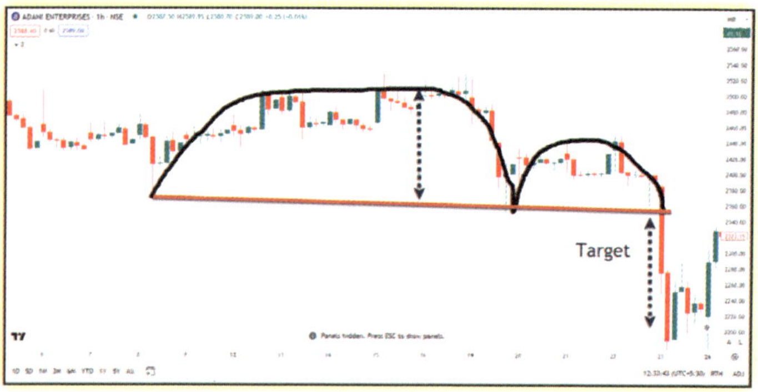

Image – Inverted Cup & Handle Pattern in Adani Ent

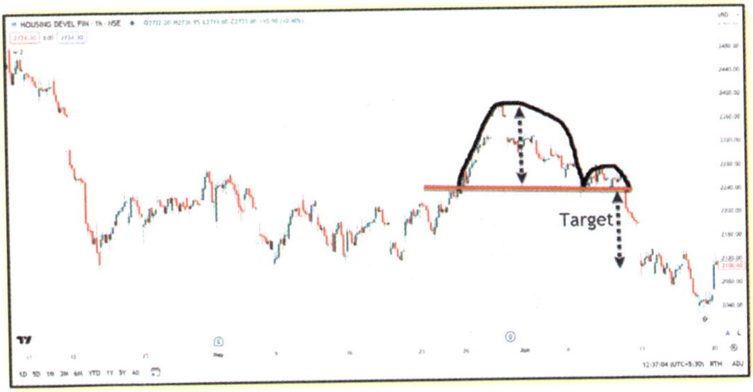

Image – Inverted Cup & Handle Pattern in HDFC

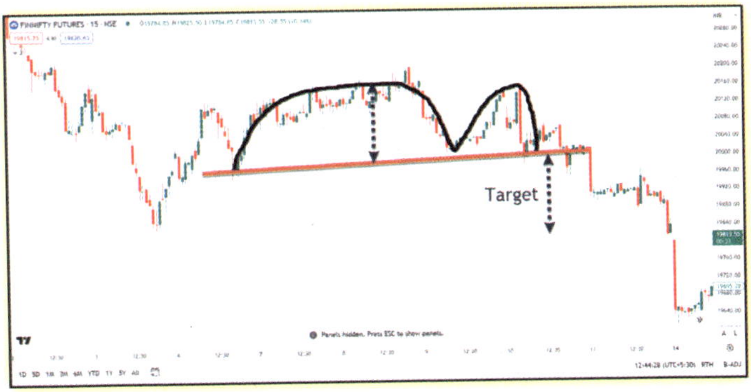

Image – Inverted Cup & Handle Pattern in Finnifty

#9 Bull Flag Pattern

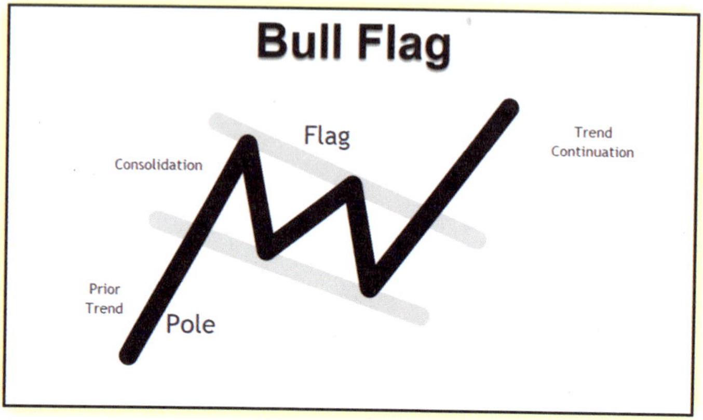

The bull flag pattern is a popular trading pattern among investors that suggests a possible continuation of an uptrend.

It's characterized by a strong upward price movement (**pole**) followed by a brief consolidation period where prices move sideways or slightly downward (**flag**).

This pattern often indicates that that price is taking a temporary pause before resuming the original upward trend.

When the price breaks out of the consolidation to the upside, it can be seen as a signal to buy, anticipating further gains.

How to Trade Bull Flag Pattern?

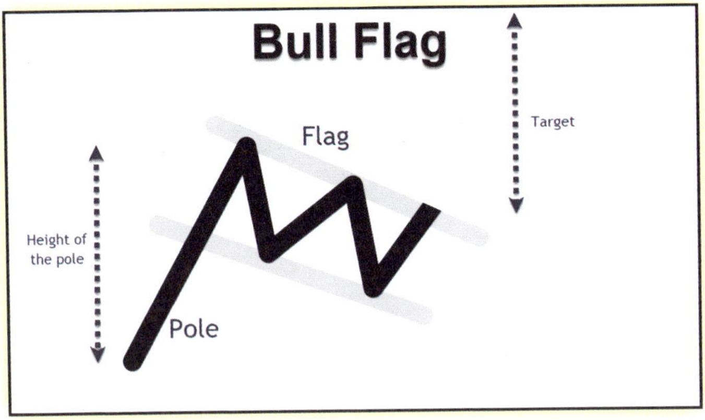

Follow the below steps to trade the bull flag pattern:

- **Identify the Flagpole**: Locate a robust upward trend price movement, which forms the flagpole.
- **Locate the Flag**: After the pole, look for a period of consolidation where the price moves sideways or slightly downward. This forms the flag portion of the pattern.
- **Entry Point**: Plan to enter a trade when the price breaks out above the upper boundary of the flag. This breakout confirms the pattern's potential continuation.
- **Set Stop-Loss**: Place a stop-loss order below the lower boundary of the flag. This helps protect your investment in case the breakout fails.
- **Target Price**: Estimate a target price by measuring the height of the flagpole and adding it to the breakout point. This gives you a rough idea of how much the price might increase.

Few Examples of Bull Flag Pattern

Image – Bull Flag Pattern in HDFC

Image – Bull Flag Pattern in SBI Life Insurance

Image – Bull Flag Pattern in Britannia Ind

Image – Bull Flag Pattern in Tech Mahindra

#10 Bear Flag Pattern

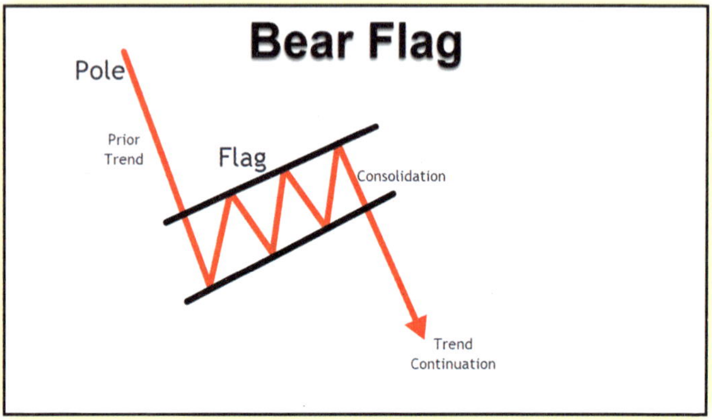

The bear flag pattern is a simple pattern that suggests a possible continuation of a downtrend.

It's the opposite of the bull flag pattern. It consists of a strong and rapid price movement (**flagpole**), followed by a small consolidation period where prices move sideways or slightly upward (**flag**).

This pattern indicates that the price is taking a breather before the downtrend resumes.

When the price breaks out of the consolidation to the downside, it can be seen as a signal to sell, anticipating further declines.

How to Trade Bear Flag Pattern?

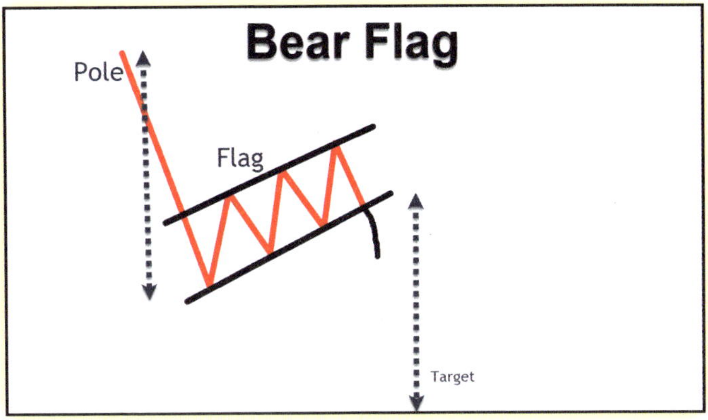

Follow the below steps to trade the bear flag pattern:

- **Identify the Flagpole**: Locate a strong downward trend price movement, which forms the flagpole.
- **Locate the Flag**: After the pole, look for a period of consolidation where the price moves sideways or slightly upside down. This forms the flag portion of the pattern.
- **Entry Point**: Plan to enter a trade when the price breaks below the lower boundary of the flag. This breakdown confirms the pattern's potential continuation.
- **Set Stop-Loss**: Place a stop-loss order above the higher boundary of the flag. This helps protect your trade in case the pattern fails.
- **Target Price**: Estimate a target price by measuring the height of the flagpole and adding it to the breakdown point. This gives you an idea of how much the price might fall further.

Few Examples of Bear Flag Pattern

Image – Bear Flag Pattern in ACC

Image – Bear Flag Pattern in Kotak Mahindra

Image – Bear Flag Pattern in Zeel

Image – Bear Flag Pattern in Nifty

#11 Symmetrical Triangle Pattern

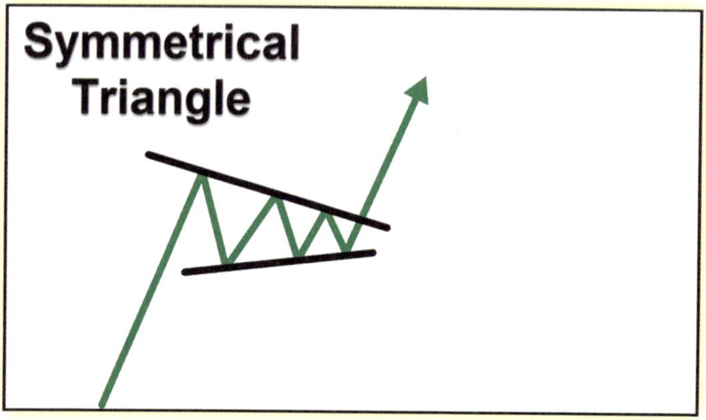

The symmetrical triangle pattern is a simple trading pattern that typically signifies a potential breakout or breakdown in price.

It's formed by converging trendlines, with lower highs and higher lows, creating a triangle shape.

This pattern highlights the indecision between buyers and sellers, and traders often anticipate a significant price move when the price breaks out of the triangle, either above the upper trendline (bullish breakout) or below the lower trendline (bearish breakdown).

How to Trade Symmetrical Triangle Pattern?

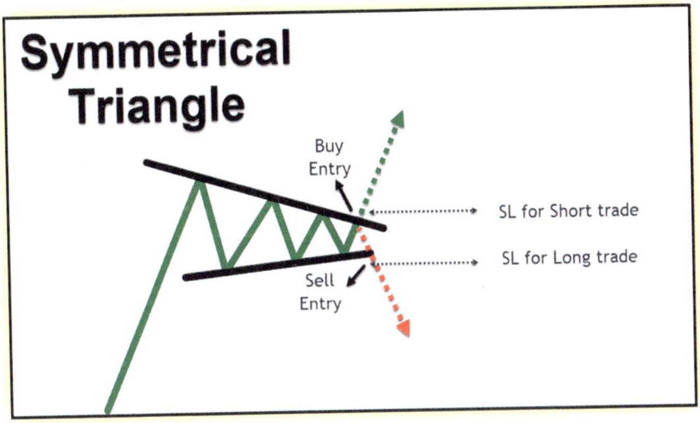

Follow the below steps to trade the symmetrical triangle pattern:

- **Identify the Triangle**: Identify the converging trendlines that form the symmetrical triangle pattern, connecting the lower highs and higher lows.
- **Wait for Breakout or Breakdown**: Monitor the price movement within the triangle. A breakout occurs when the price breaches the upper trendline (bullish breakout) or breaks the lower trendline (bearish breakdown).
- **Entry Point**: If there's a bullish breakout, consider entering a buy trade as the price moves above the upper trendline. Consider entering a sell trade for a bearish breakdown as the price moves below the lower trendline.

- **Stop-Loss Placement**: Set a stop-loss order just beyond the opposite side of the breakout point to limit potential losses if the breakout fails.
- **Target Price**: Estimate a target price by measuring the height of the widest part of the triangle and adding it to the breakout point (for a bullish breakout) or subtracting it (for a bearish breakdown).

Few Examples of Symmetrical Triangle Pattern

Image – Symmetrical Triangle Pattern in Banknifty

Image – Symmetrical Triangle Pattern in Nifty

Image – Symmetrical Triangle Pattern in Reliance

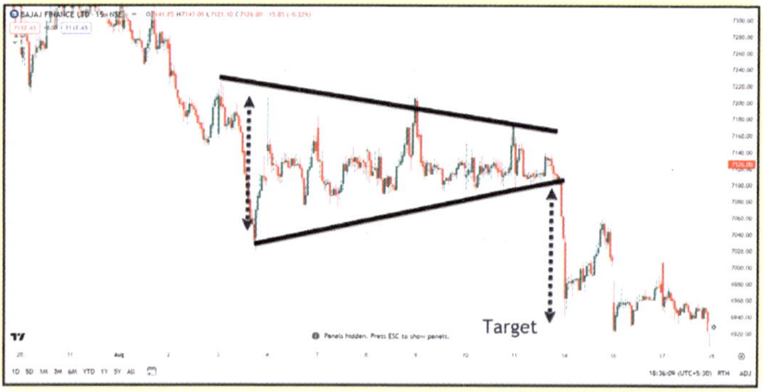

Image – Symmetrical Triangle Pattern in Bajaj Finance

#12 Rising Wedge Pattern

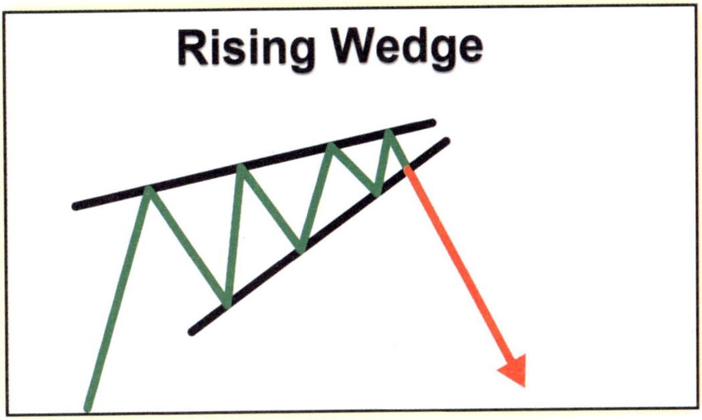

The rising wedge pattern is a simple chart pattern that often indicates a potential reversal in an uptrend.

It's formed by converging trend lines that slope upward, with higher highs and higher lows. This pattern suggests weakening bullish momentum as the price consolidates within the narrowing range.

Traders often anticipate a breakdown to the downside, leading to a possible downtrend, when the price breaks below the lower trend line of the wedge.

How to Trade Rising Wedge Trading Pattern?

Follow the below steps to trade the rising wedge pattern:

- **Identify the Rising Wedge**: Identify the converging trend lines that form the rising wedge pattern, with higher highs and higher lows.
- **Watch for Breakdown**: Monitor the price as it approaches the apex of the wedge. Look for a breakdown to the downside, where the price breaks below the lower trend line.
- **Entry Point**: If there is a breakdown, consider entering a short trade as the price moves below the lower trend line.
- **Stop-Loss Placement**: Set a stop-loss order just above the upper trend line of the wedge to limit potential losses if the breakdown fails.
- **Target Price**: Estimate a target price by measuring the height of the widest part of the wedge and subtracting it from the breakdown point.

Few Examples of Rising Wedge Pattern

Image – Rising Wedge Pattern in HDFC

Image – Rising Wedge Pattern in Bajaj Finance

Image – Rising Wedge Pattern in Infosys

Image – Rising Wedge Pattern in IOC

Candlestick Patterns

#1 Bullish Engulfing Pattern

The bullish engulfing pattern is a candlestick pattern often signals a potential trend reversal from bearish to bullish.

It occurs when a smaller bearish candle is followed by a larger bullish candle that completely engulfs the previous range of the candle.

This pattern indicates that the selling pressure is reducing, and buyers are taking control, potentially leading to an uptrend.

Traders often see the bullish engulfing pattern as a signal to buy or go long.

Few Examples of Bullish Engulfing Pattern

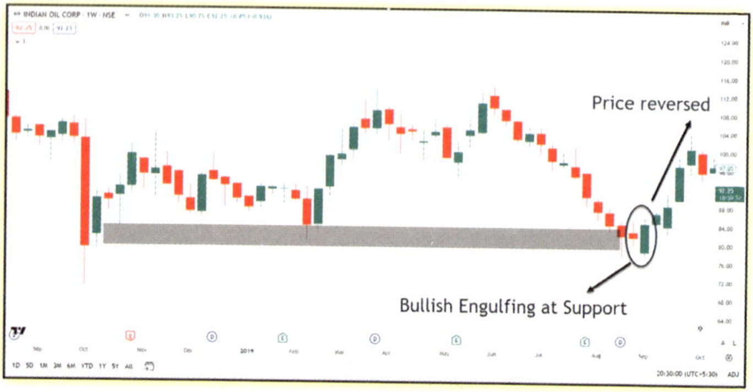

Image – Bullish Engulfing Pattern in IOC

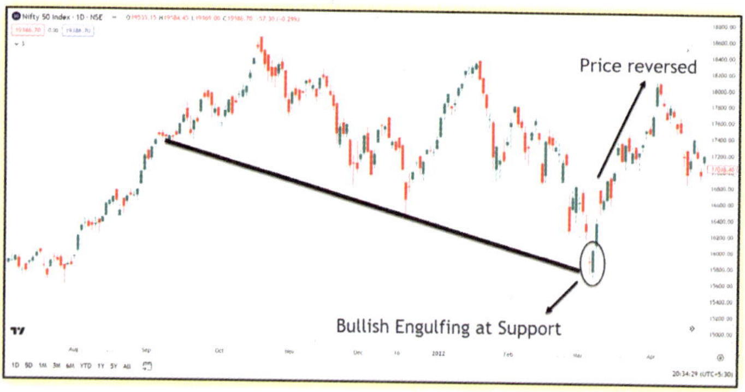

Image – Bullish Engulfing Pattern in Nifty

#2 Bearish Engulfing Pattern

The bearish engulfing pattern is a candlestick pattern that often indicates a potential trend reversal from bullish to bearish.

It happens when a smaller bullish candle is followed by a larger bearish candle that completely engulfs the previous range of the candle.

This pattern suggests that buying momentum is decreasing, and sellers are gaining control, potentially leading to a downtrend.

Traders often interpret the bearish engulfing pattern as a signal to sell or go short.

Few Examples of Bearish Engulfing Pattern

Image – Bearish Engulfing Pattern in Nifty

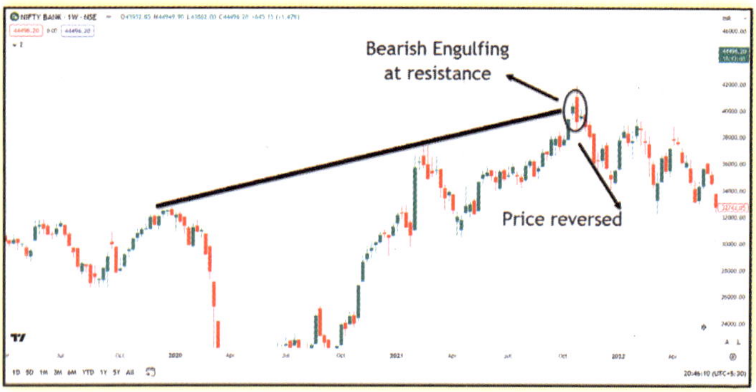

Image – Bearish Engulfing Pattern in Banknifty

#3 Marubozu Pattern

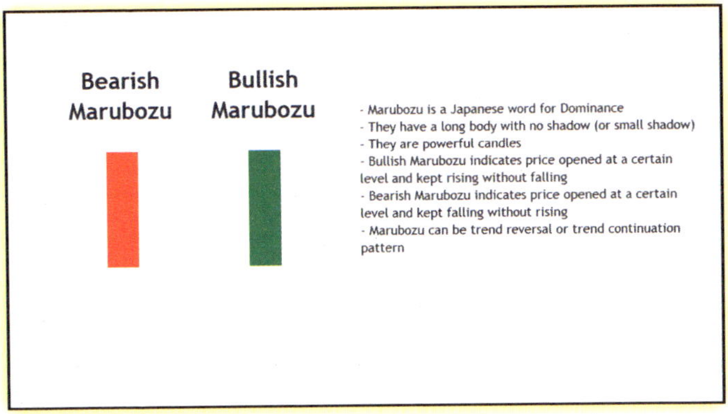

The marubozu pattern is a candlestick pattern in the technical analysis world characterized by a single candle with little to no wicks.

There are two types: bullish and bearish.

A bullish marubozu has no upper wick and indicates **strong buying** throughout the trading session, suggesting a potential uptrend continuation.

A bearish marubozu has no lower wick and indicates **strong selling**, indicating a possible downtrend continuation.

These patterns are often considered as signals of strong market sentiment and can help traders anticipate future price movements.

Few Examples of Bullish Marubozu Pattern

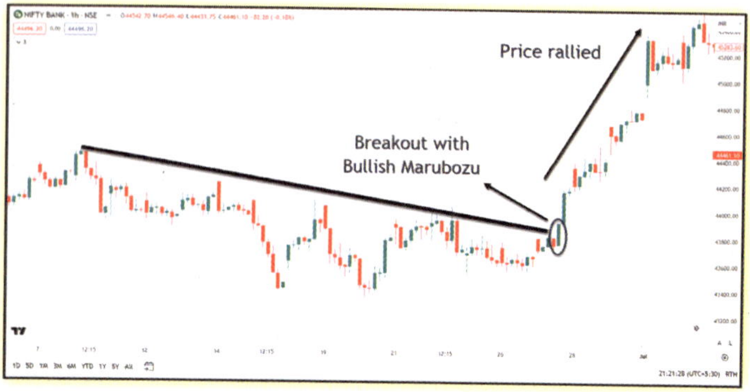

Image – Bullish Marubozu Pattern in Banknifty

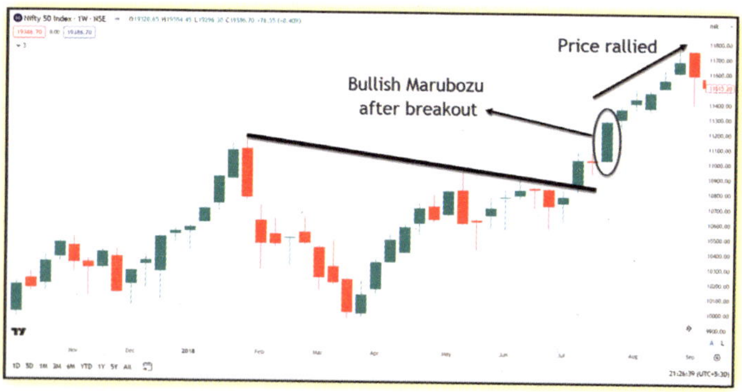

Image – Bullish Marubozu Pattern in Nifty

Few Examples of Bearish Marubozu Pattern

Image – Bearish Marubozu Pattern in Nifty

Image – Bearish Marubozu Pattern in Banknifty

#4 Pinbar Pattern

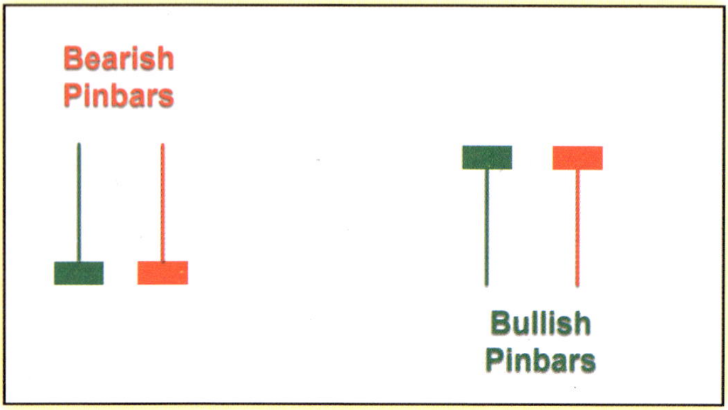

The pinbar, a short form of "**Pinocchio bar**," is a candlestick pattern in trading that often signals a potential trend reversal, either upside or downside.

It consists of a single candle with a small body and a long wick, either above or below the body. The wick represents a rejection of price at a certain level.

A bullish pinbar has a long lower wick (either with a green or red body) and suggests potential buying after a decline.

A bearish pinbar has a long upper wick (either with a green or red body) and indicates potential selling after a rise.

Few Examples of Bullish Pinbar Pattern

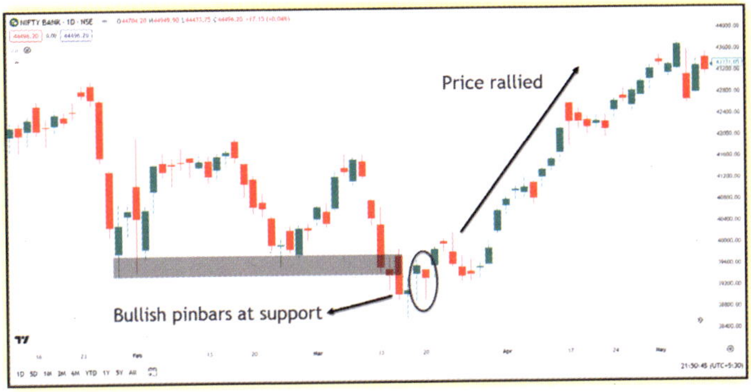

Image – Bullish Pinbar Pattern in Banknifty

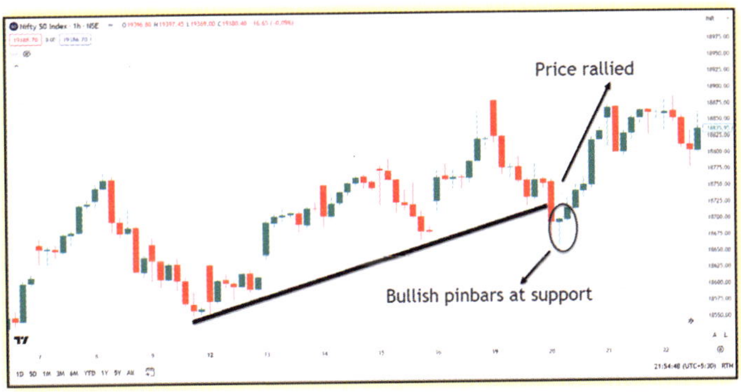

Image – Bullish Pinbar Pattern in Nifty

Few Examples of Bearish Pinbar Pattern

Image – Bullish Pinbar Pattern in Finnifty

Image – Bullish Pinbar Pattern in Reliance

#5 Doji Pattern

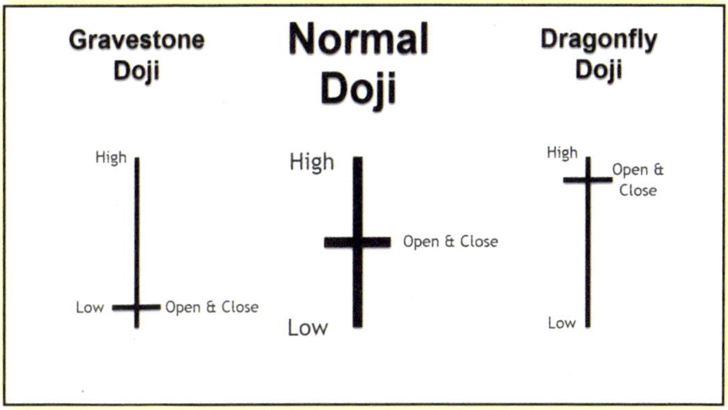

The doji is a simple candlestick pattern in trading that signifies **indecision** in the market.

This pattern forms when the opening and closing prices of a candlestick are very close or at the same price levels, creating a small or non-existent body with a long wick.

Doji patterns can have various interpretations:

- **Neutral Doji (Normal Doji):** When the open and close prices are at the same levels and very close to the center price range, it indicates market indecision.
- **Dragonfly Doji**: A doji with a long lower wick can suggest a potential uptrend reversal, indicating buyers' participation after a decline.
- **Gravestone Doji**: A doji with a long upper wick can suggest a potential downtrend reversal, indicating sellers entering the market after an uptrend.

Usually, traders often view doji patterns as signals to pay attention to upcoming price movements near support and resistance levels and consider them in conjunction with other indicators to make informed trading decisions.

Few Examples of Doji Pattern

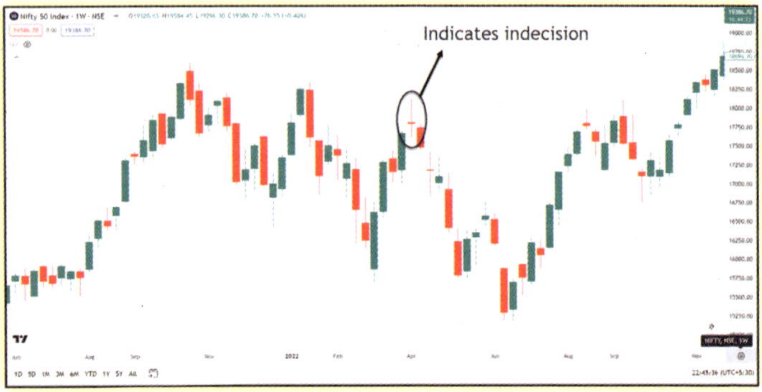

Image – Doji Pattern in Nifty

Image – Gravestone Doji Pattern in Banknifty

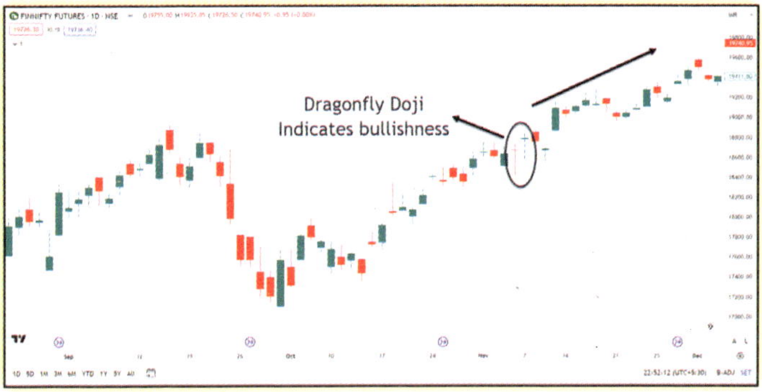

Image – Dragonfly Doji Pattern in Finnifty

A Word of Caution!

Using chart patterns and candlestick patterns in trading can be beneficial, but it's essential to exercise caution and follow certain precautions to avoid common pitfalls.

Here are some detailed precautions to consider:

- **Confirmation**: Do not rely solely on a single pattern when making trading decisions. Use chart patterns and candlestick patterns in combination with other technical indicators, fundamental analysis, and market trends to confirm signals.
- **False Signals**: Please understand that not all patterns lead to successful trading. False signals can occur due to market noise or sudden news events. Always be prepared for possible losses.
- **Timeframes**: Analyze patterns across different timeframes to ensure consistency. What looks like a vital pattern in a short timeframe can be a small noise in a long timeframe.
- **Practice and Learning**: Do not participate in actual trading based only on theoretical knowledge. Practice using patterns on a demo

account or small positions until you gain confidence and experience.

- **Risk Management**: Set stop-loss orders to determine your risk tolerance and protect against unexpected price movements. Do not risk more than you can afford to lose on a single trade.
- **Pattern Size**: The size of the pattern matters. Larger patterns tend to have more significance and reliability compared to smaller ones.
- **Pattern Completion**: Wait until the pattern is fully developed and check before taking action. Entering prematurely may result in losses if patterns change or fail to materialize.
- **Volume**: Consider trading volume when analyzing patterns. High volume during a pattern's breakout can provide more conviction in the validity of the signal.
- **Market Context**: Analyze the overall market situation. A pattern formed in a strong trend may have a different impact than the same pattern in a volatile market.
- **Psychology**: Understand the psychology behind these trading patterns. Patterns reflect the emotions and behavior of market participants. So, consider the psychology of other traders when interpreting patterns.
- **Patience**: Be patient and choose carefully. Not all patterns can be traded, and forced trades can result in losses. Wait for the high-probability setups.

- **Continuous Learning**: Markets evolve, and the meaning of patterns can change over time. Stay informed and keep up to date with the latest market trends.
- **Backtesting**: Test historical data to see how well a particular pattern performed under different market conditions. This will give you an idea of the reliability of the pattern.
- **Avoid Overtrading**: Avoid trading too frequently or overleveraging. Quality over quantity is crucial when using patterns.
- **Adaptation**: Be prepared to adapt your trading strategy to changing market conditions. What works for one market type may not work for another market type.

Please note that trading involves risk, and no strategy guarantees profit. Chart patterns and candlestick patterns provide valuable insight, but combining them with careful risk management and a well thought out trading plan is important.

Importance of Money Management

Whenever a trader takes a trade, it can only have any one of the below five outcomes:

1. A breakeven
2. A small profit
3. A small loss
4. A big profit
5. **A BIG LOSS**

Except for the 5th point, all other outcomes allow us to survive in the trading business. However, losing big on any trade is an unacceptable sin in trading.

> ***"I have two basic rules about winning in trading as well as in life: 1. If you don't bet, you can't win. 2. If you lose all your chips, you can't bet."***
>
> – Larry Hite

The above quote alone explains the importance of money management in trading. This is an important skill that directly affects your trading account.

Even with a great technical system, poor money management can lead to all sorts of unwanted errors that can lead to account explosions.

Below are the critical aspects of money management:

- **Risk Control**: Money management allows you to limit the amount of capital you risk on a single trade and prevent significant losses that could jeopardize your trading account.
- **Capital Preservation**: Effective money management allows you to maintain your trading capital in the long term and to continue trading after setbacks.
- **Emotional Discipline**: Following a well-defined money management plan can reduce the influence of emotions such as fear and greed on your trading decisions.
- **Consistency**: Proper money management promotes consistency in trading approaches, prevents erratic behavior, and ensures the maintenance of stable strategies.
- **Long-Term Growth**: Through careful position sizing and risk management, money management avoids excessive losses and maximizes profits, laying the foundation for stable long-term growth.

The Importance of Trading Psychology

Good trading psychology is essential for success in trading because it directly impacts your decision-making process, risk management, and overall performance.

Here's why it matters:

- **Emotion Management**: Trading can be an emotional challenge. Good trading psychology helps you manage emotions such as fear, greed, impatience and prevents making impulsive decisions that can lead to losses.
- **Disciplined Execution**: Maintaining a strong psychological mindset can help in protecting your trading plans and strategies even during heightened market volatility and uncertainty.
- **Objective Decision-Making**: A healthy trading psychology helps you make decisions based on analysis and strategy rather than emotional reactions, leading to more objective and informed decisions.
- **Risk Management**: Effective trading psychology helps you adopt appropriate risk management techniques and maintain your risk

tolerance so that you do not take excessive risks based on your emotional impulses.

- **Adaptability**: The market is constantly changing. A healthy trading psychology will help you adapt to changing market conditions and avoid the frustration of rigid thinking.
- **Learning from Mistakes**: A positive psychological approach sees losses and failures as learning opportunities rather than failures, leading to continuous improvement and growth.
- **Confidence**: Confident traders make rational decisions and stick to their strategies. Good trading psychology builds confidence in one's abilities, leading to better performance.
- **Reduced Stress**: Trading can be stressful, but with a solid psychological foundation, you can handle stress well and maintain focus and clarity during difficult times.
- **Long-Term Success**: Trading is a journey. A good trading psychology can help you navigate the ups and downs and avoid the common pitfalls that lead to early exit so you can stay in the trade for the long term.
- **Consistent Performance**: A balanced state of mind contributes to consistent trading performance, allowing you to execute your strategies over the long term consistently.
- In summary, trading is not just about charts and numbers. It's about mastering your own psychology. Developing resilience and a disciplined mindset is just as important as

learning technical and fundamental analysis. Without good trading psychology, even the most promising strategies can fail.

Dear Readers,

My heartfelt congratulations to each of you as you read my book and embark on your journey into the fascinating world of stock market trading.

May the knowledge and insights within these pages give you the tools to navigate the complexity of your markets with confidence and wisdom.

Remember that trading success is not just numbers. Understanding psychology, managing risk, and making informed decisions is key.

I hope this book provided inspiration, guidance, and practical strategies for achieving your financial goals.

May your trading business be profitable, your learning journey be prosperous. Aim for success in stock exchange trading!

If you have any questions, reach me on Indrazith.com

Discover the next level of trading insights and strategies in "**How to Make Money with Breakout Trading**" book – a must-read for those ready to take their understanding to new heights and unlock further success.

Best regards,
Indrazith Shantharaj

Other titles by Indrazith Shantharaj,
published by Manjul Publishing House

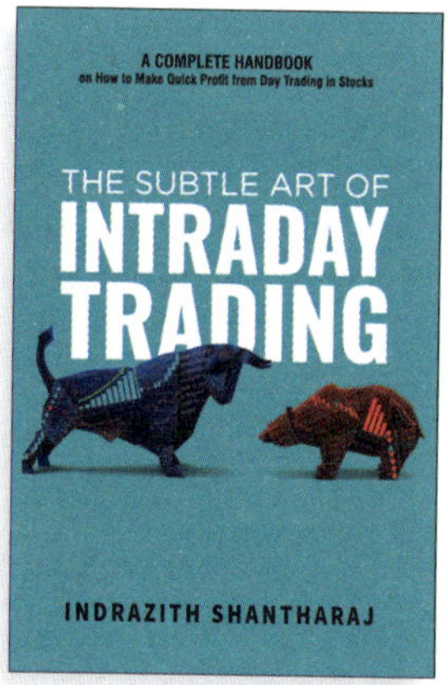